Take a journey with me

"A weight loss journal to document your weight loss journey"

By

Theresa Mitchell

Dedication

This book is dedicated to my amazing children, whom I love so dearly.

To Tashira, my first born and only girl: From the moment I looked in your eyes, I knew that I had to change my life for you so that I could make you proud. The childhood I had was very difficult, and I knew that once I had you, I didn't want you to have the same difficulties that I had. So, I knew that opening up my own salon would teach you that we are Bosses in this family and that you can do anything you put your mind to. You don't have to just work at the salon; you can own one. I've been a salon owner for over 16 years. I love you, daughter, and I'm thankful that I made many sacrifices for you. You show me each and every day that I chose the right path. You are so smart, beautiful, and caring; you are definitely my mini-me. Thank you for your sweetness and understanding as we travel through life together. I know it's difficult being my daughter some days because mommy is very busy helping everybody else, but it's easy loving you because you get me like no other. Thank you for blessing me with my first granddaughter, Thyri' Ilise, whom I adore deeply. You both are my inspiration.

To my oldest son, Jachin, my deep thinker, my college graduate, my business partner: What more can I say? Getting your bachelor's degree in psychology from The University of Michigan Ann Arbor campus was one of the biggest highlights of my life because I know how hard you worked to get there and the sacrifices you made to finish school. For that, I'm forever proud of you and forever grateful to be your mom. You have taught me some amazing lessons, and I'm blessed to have a front-row seat witnessing your greatness. I salute you for being a great role model for your brothers, and I appreciate all that you do.

To my middle son, Joshua, the artist (like me), the athlete (like me), the business owner (like me): Oh my goodness, I created a male version of myself, and I love it. Joshua, the way you started your barber career just like me is unbelievable. To be a self-taught barber who's grown their client list in one year is remarkable; I am so proud. The way we bond is like no other. The 5k runs and the half marathon runs we go on are the best bonding experiences for us, and I wouldn't change that for anything in this world. I'm blessed to receive medals with you and share these great memories together. I can't wait to see how far you go in the business, but I'm blessed to sit in the passenger seat as you drive on this road called life. Congratulations to you, son.

To my dearest Julian, the baby of the family: Oh, how I love you. You are my twin flame, always by my side. Whether we are at bootcamp at The G.O.A.T Locker room or in the kitchen cooking family meals, you are always by my side. I love how you can break down any situation and see the good in it; it makes my heart smile. Your heart is pure, and your love runs deep, and I'm so proud of you. Each day, you show me what it means to love unconditionally.

Acknowledgment

First and foremost, I give honor to God, who is the head of my life. There would be no me without You, and for that, I am eternally grateful. My spiritual walk is incredibly important to me, and I give all praise to the Most High.

I would like to thank my mommy, Helen Moody. She loves to write, and I've noticed that since I've been taking care of her these past seven years, all she does is write. She fills countless notebooks with her thoughts and feelings, which she calls her "books." Mommy, you are the reason I continue to write. I never knew we shared this love for writing until you got sick. Thank you for being my inspiration.

My grandparents, Leamon Jones and Elizabeth Johnson, are my world. Though they are no longer here in person, they are always with me in spirit. My grandfather, Lieutenant Colonel Leamon Jones, taught me the importance of keeping my word to myself, and I am thankful that he instilled that value in me. Granddad, I am here, keeping my word and standing on business, just like you taught me.

To my goddaughter, one of my biggest fans (and I am hers), thank you for always running ideas by me to make sure they make sense and for saving me money. You ensure I'm organized and not overwhelmed, despite the busy life of being a hairstylist, mentor, writer, daughter, mom, and grandmother. Katrice, I couldn't do it without your assistance and encouragement. I love you.

I would also like to thank my personal trainers, Marcell and James, at The G.O.A.T Locker Room in Redford, Michigan. I've worked with many personal trainers over the years, but these young men have taught me to understand my body and what is best for me. I've never been this confident in my fitness abilities until now, and I appreciate them for simply being themselves.

A huge shoutout to my running buddy, Robert Samuels. Without him, I'm sure I would still be running only on the riverfront. Robert introduced me to different 5K and 10K runs and connected me with other runners, and now we have a village. I am now the proud holder of 20 medals (20 runs so far), with more to come. Thank you for being my inspiration, Robert. I appreciate you.

In the summer of 2024, I was blessed to assist another runner, Whitney, in organizing our very first 5K run for our Juneteenth event, in conjunction with the official Juneteenth festival coordinator, Kong. We had such a great turnout, and I am grateful that Kong and Whitney believed in me. The event was a success, and I am thankful for the opportunity.

Last but not least, I want to thank my little sister, Diamond, owner of "D's Eats," who is also my private chef. She teaches me about clean eating and makes the best healthy meals for me to try, and yes, they are delicious. I am blessed to have a handful of amazing people in my life on this journey. I would be lost without them, and for that, I am forever grateful.

Contents

About the Author

Theresa Mitchell is my name, and I've always had childhood dreams of becoming a writer. I used to write all the time, but as I got older, that flame fizzled away. I found my newest passion that I would love also. At 12 years old, I found myself styling hair. By the time I reached 14 years old, I had started building my client list and had become a busy hairstylist practicing on my family, friends, and neighbors in my neighborhood.

I began beauty school at 20 years old, right after I had my first child, my daughter. As soon as I got into the groove of beauty school, I became pregnant with my second child. I quickly understood that if this was something I really wanted to do, I had to push through any obstacles that may come my way to get it done, and that I did. I knew that this was what I wanted to do with my life. A few years and one more child later, I became a licensed hairstylist, and I opened up my first salon in January 2006.

I wanted to open up my own salon because I wanted to teach my daughter that you can run your own business from right behind your chair. I wanted her to know that you are the boss of your own life, and you can go far in this world if you want. Being a salon owner put me in the perfect position to mentor young girls as they needed to make a few dollars and needed someone to be a listening ear, and I was blessed to help many.

In the winter of 2020, my daughter came to me with the idea of helping more girls at one time instead of one by one. The only way I thought this could happen was to start a nonprofit organization where I mentor a group of girls at one time. Here we are in 2024, still going strong. The Young Sistaz Elite club has really changed my life. To be able to help out over 200 young girls over the course of four years is amazing, and for that, I am very proud. In the summer of 2021, we started our boys' organization, The Young Brothaz Elite Club, led by my oldest son, Jachin.

As I mentor the children monthly, I get a chance to grow myself and tap into who I really am. With this newfound sense of happiness and becoming more of a giver of my time, life as I knew it had changed, and I decided to go on my journey of growing and understanding who I really am. I started to feel this void in my life that I couldn't understand until I picked up my pen.

See, as a child, I always got great grades in writing and English classes because I loved writing. So, once I started to write this first book, I felt free and happy. I now understand more about myself. I believe in myself more because I'm doing something that I've loved doing since I was a child. I'm so blessed that I unlocked the little girl inside of me and began to write my very first book. I pray that this book brings you the joy while reading and doing the exercises that it gave me as I wrote it. You are helping a young girl's dreams come true. Thank you forever, and please continue to look out for more of my journeys.

Introduction to the Journey

My life is like a long road trip filled with adventures, challenges, and beautiful moments. Along the way, I've taken many detours and side trips, each one adding something special to my story.

One of the most important journeys I've embarked on is my health journey. It's like a path I walk every day, making choices that affect how I feel and how I live. This journey isn't always easy, but it's gratifying.

It all started when I realized that taking care of my body and mind was essential for living a happy life. I began by making small changes, like eating healthier foods and moving my body more. It wasn't always smooth sailing. There were bumps in the road, like temptations to eat junk food or days when I didn't feel like exercising. But I kept going, reminding myself of the destination: a healthier, happier me.

As I continued on this journey, I discovered so much about myself. I learned that self-discipline and perseverance are key ingredients to success. I also found joy in discovering new recipes, trying different forms of exercise, and feeling more robust and energetic.

But it wasn't just about physical health; my mental and emotional well-being also improved. I found ways to manage stress and practice self-care, like meditation and spending time in nature. These small changes had a significant impact on my overall happiness and fulfillment.

Now, my health journey is an integral part of who I am. It's not just about reaching a certain weight or fitting into a specific size; it's about feeling confident, vibrant, and alive. And while the journey never truly ends, I'm grateful for every step I've taken and every lesson I've learned along the way.

Back in 2019, when everything seemed pretty normal for everyone else, a big challenge came knocking at my door. At that time, I was a 39-year-old mom taking care of four kids, all born through C-sections. Let me tell you, those C-sections left me with a lot of tummy troubles.

My doctor, seeing the state of my health, suggested something I never thought I'd need: a hysterectomy. Honestly, I was not thrilled about it. Who would be, right? Surgery is scary stuff. But the truth was, I was dealing with more than just a few tummy issues. It turned out my condition was pretty serious.

So, with a mix of sadness and frustration, I went under the knife. But here's the twist: after the surgery, I felt like a whole new person. I mean, I was happy and relieved! It turns out that the surgery was a real lifesaver. My doctor told me that my condition was way worse than he initially thought. Without the surgery, I would've been in years of pain and trouble.

That experience changed everything for me. It made me realize how important it is to listen to your body and trust the experts. From that day forward, I knew my life would never be the same. I had a new appreciation for my health and a fresh perspective on life.

Sure, it wasn't an easy journey. Surgery never is. But looking back, I'm grateful for every step of it.

My fitness journey began more than two decades ago, back in the year 2000, just after welcoming my first child into the world – my daughter, born in April. From the start, I was what you might call a "gym girl." I knew the ins and outs of hard work and dedication when it came to my workouts.

Fast forward to January 2020. After going through a hysterectomy and taking the time to heal, I realized that this time around, things were different. I wasn't just hitting the gym to stay in shape; I was fighting for my life. Being older now, every workout felt like a crucial step towards my health and well-being.

Despite the challenges ahead, I embraced this journey with gratitude. I knew it wouldn't be easy, but I was determined to make every day count. And I want you to join me on this beautiful journey.

So, let's kick things off with a 90-day personal guide to a healthier you. Together, we'll take small steps each day toward our goals. Whether it's hitting the gym, trying out new recipes, or practicing mindfulness, we'll do it together every step of the way.

I'm excited to share this journey with you because I believe that together, we can achieve anything. So, lace up your sneakers, grab a water bottle, and start this adventure toward better health and happiness.

Invitation for readers to join in the health journey.

Every morning, as the sun peeks through my window, I embark on a ritual that sets the tone for my entire day: breakfast and a Bible verse. It's a simple yet powerful routine that I've followed for years, and I'd love for you to join me on this journey towards better health and spiritual well-being.

Let's talk about breakfast first. Did you know that breakfast is often referred to as the most important meal of the day? It's not just a saying; it's backed by science. Studies have shown that eating breakfast can kickstart your metabolism, improve concentration and focus, and even help with weight management. Research published in the American Journal of Clinical Nutrition found that people who eat breakfast tend to have healthier overall diets and are less likely to be overweight or obese.

But it's not just about any breakfast; it's about making healthy choices. Incorporating whole grains, fruits, and lean proteins into your morning meal can provide essential nutrients and energy to fuel your day. So, whether it's a bowl of oatmeal topped with fresh berries, whole-grain toast with avocado, or a smoothie packed with greens and protein, aim to start your day with a nutritious breakfast.

Now, let's add a sprinkle of inspiration to our morning routine with a motivational Bible verse. Jeremiah 33:6 reminds us, "Nevertheless, I will bring health and healing to it; I will heal my people and will let them enjoy abundant peace and security." This verse serves as a reminder of the importance of prioritizing our health and well-being, both physically and spiritually.

By incorporating a nutritious breakfast and a motivational Bible verse into our mornings, we're setting ourselves up for success in all aspects of our lives. We're nourishing our bodies with the fuel they need to thrive, and we're feeding our souls with words of encouragement and faith.

So, I invite you to join me in this health journey. Let's commit to starting each day with a wholesome breakfast and a dose of inspiration from the Word of God. Together, we can cultivate healthy habits that will nourish our bodies, minds, and spirits for years to come.

Before & After Journey

Space is left intentionally so that readers can insert their pictures.

Let me tell you about a powerful tool I've discovered on my health journey: before and after photos. These snapshots capture more than just physical changes; they reflect a journey of transformation, motivation, and reflection. I want to share with you why these photos are so important and how they've helped me stay focused on my goals.

First off, let's talk about why before and after photos are crucial in tracking progress. When we're in the midst of our journey, it's easy to get caught up in the day-to-day fluctuations of weight and measurements. But photos provide a visual record of our progress that numbers alone can't capture. They show us how far we've come, even on days when the scale doesn't budge, or the tape measure doesn't move.

Looking back at my own before and after photos, I'm reminded of the power of patience and persistence. It's not always easy to stay motivated, especially when progress feels slow or stalled. But seeing the tangible evidence of my hard work in those photos keeps me going. It reminds me that every healthy choice, every workout, every moment of self-discipline is worth it in the end.

And here's the thing: progress isn't just about the numbers on a scale or a measuring tape. It's about how we feel, how we carry ourselves, and how we see ourselves in the mirror. Losing inches and gaining confidence is impressive, but it's also about feeling more potent, energized, and alive.

So, I want to encourage you to embrace the practice of taking before and after photos on your journey. It may feel a little awkward at first, but trust me, it's worth it. Find a comfortable place with good lighting, put on an outfit you feel good in, and snap those pics. And don't worry about being perfect; this is about progress, not perfection.

As you continue on your journey, remember to be patient with yourself. Rome wasn't built in a day, and neither is a healthy lifestyle. It takes time, effort, and consistency. But with each step forward, each healthy choice, you're moving closer to your goals.

Celebrate your victories, no matter how small, and use those photos as a reminder of how far you've come. And remember, keep pushing forward, stay focused on your goals, and believe in yourself. You've got this!

Get in the gym

Hitting the gym wasn't just about looking good or staying fit. It was about something much bigger - it was about fighting for my life.

See, as I got older, every workout felt like it could make a massive difference in my health and how I felt overall. It wasn't just about lifting weights or running on the treadmill. It was about taking care of myself urgently and essentially.

So, there I was, back in the gym, putting in the work like never before. Every rep, every sweat session, felt like I was pushing towards something significant - my well-being. And let me tell you, it wasn't easy. There were days when I felt tired and wanted to stay in bed and skip the gym altogether. But I knew deep down that I had to keep going. My health depended on it.

And you know what? Over time, I started to feel stronger, both physically and mentally. Each workout wasn't just about getting through it; it was about proving to myself that I could do it, that I was capable of taking control of my health and my life.

Looking back, I can see how much I've grown since those early days in the gym. Back then, I was just a new mom trying to stay in shape. Now, I'm a fighter, someone who knows the importance of taking care of themselves, no matter what life throws their way.

So, here I am, still hitting the gym, still pushing myself to be the best version of myself that I can be. Because when it comes down to it, my health and well-being are worth fighting for every single day.

Workout Schedule and Accountability

Now, in this book, you can jot down all your favorite exercises. Think of it as creating your own little space where you promise to look after yourself and stay pumped up to keep going.

So, what kind of exercises do you like? Maybe you're into jogging or lifting weights. Or perhaps you prefer yoga or dancing. Whatever it is, could you write it down in this book? Make it your go-to guide for staying active and feeling great.

The key here is consistency. Committing to working out at least four times a week allows your body to get more vital and energized. And hey, it's not just about the physical benefits. Exercise is also great for your mental health, helping you feel happier and more focused.

Emphasis on the significance of regular exercise

In the journey towards a healthier and happier life, regular exercise stands as an indispensable ally. Its significance reverberates not only through physical health but also mental and emotional well-being. Let's embark on a journey to explore the transformative power of regular exercise through tangible statistics, figures, and easy-to-understand language.

Physical Health Benefits:

Regular exercise serves as a cornerstone in the fortress of physical health. Statistics reveal that engaging in moderate-intensity aerobic activity for at least 150 minutes per week can significantly reduce the risk of chronic diseases such as heart disease, diabetes, and certain types of cancer. Furthermore, it aids in weight management by burning calories and boosting metabolism.

According to recent figures, individuals who exercise regularly are 50% less likely to experience obesity-related health issues compared to sedentary counterparts.

Moreover, the benefits extend to musculoskeletal health. Strength training exercises not only increase muscle mass and strength but also enhance bone density, reducing the risk of osteoporosis. Studies indicate that adults who engage in strength training at least twice a week experience a 20-30% reduction in the risk of fractures.

Mental and Emotional Well-being:

Beyond the physical realm, regular exercise exerts a profound impact on mental and emotional well-being. Figures demonstrate that physical activity stimulates the release of endorphins, neurotransmitters responsible for feelings of happiness and euphoria. This natural mood lift can alleviate symptoms of anxiety and depression, with research indicating that exercise is as effective as medication in treating mild to moderate depression.

Furthermore, engaging in regular exercise fosters cognitive function and brain health. Studies reveal that individuals who exercise regularly experience improved memory, attention, and overall mental performance. This cognitive boost is attributed to increased blood flow to the brain, which promotes the growth of new brain cells and enhances neural connectivity.

Quality of Life:

The transformative power of regular exercise extends beyond health outcomes, enriching the quality of life in myriad ways. Statistics indicate that individuals who engage in regular physical activity report higher levels of energy and vitality, enabling them to participate more fully in daily activities and pursuits. Moreover, regular exercise promotes better sleep quality, with figures showing that active individuals are 65% less likely to experience insomnia symptoms.

Furthermore, the social aspect of exercise contributes to overall well-being. Whether through group fitness classes, sports teams, or outdoor activities, exercise provides opportunities for social interaction and connection, fostering a sense of belonging and community. Studies indicate that individuals with strong social ties experience better mental health and overall life satisfaction.

Empowerment and Resilience:

Embracing a regimen of regular exercise is not merely a journey toward physical fitness but a pathway to empowerment and resilience. Figures reveal that individuals who exercise regularly demonstrate greater self-confidence and self-esteem as they witness their bodies' capabilities and accomplishments. This sense of empowerment transcends the gym or fitness studio, permeating into various aspects of life, from professional endeavors to personal relationships.

Moreover, regular exercise cultivates resilience in the face of adversity. By overcoming physical challenges and pushing past perceived limitations, individuals develop a resilient mindset that equips them to tackle life's obstacles with courage and determination. Studies indicate that regular exercisers are better equipped to cope with stress and bounce back from setbacks, showcasing the profound psychological benefits of an active lifestyle.

11

Encouragement to work out at least 4 days a week

Let's delve into the compelling reasons why dedicating yourself to at least four days of exercise each week can transform your life.

Physical Health Amplified:

Picture this: four days a week, engaging in purposeful physical activity that nourishes your body and strengthens your foundation of health. Research consistently demonstrates that this level of commitment significantly reduces the risk of chronic diseases such as heart disease, diabetes, and certain cancers. By investing in your health through regular exercise, you're not just adding years to your life, but life to your years.

Furthermore, a four-day workout routine provides ample opportunities to diversify your exercise regimen, incorporating elements of cardiovascular training, strength training, flexibility work, and even restorative practices like yoga or tai chi. This holistic approach ensures that every facet of your physical fitness is nurtured, leading to a resilient and capable body that can thrive in the face of life's challenges.

Mental Fortitude Forged:

The benefits of a four-day workout routine extend far beyond the physical realm, permeating into the realm of mental fortitude and emotional resilience. Engaging in regular exercise stimulates the release of endorphins, those magical neurotransmitters that flood your system with feelings of joy and well-being. By prioritizing your mental health through consistent physical activity, you're equipping yourself with a powerful tool to navigate life's inevitable ups and downs with grace and resilience.

Moreover, the discipline and commitment required to maintain a four-day workout routine cultivate a mindset of perseverance and determination that spills over into every aspect of your life. When you show up for yourself on the gym floor or the running trail four days a week, you're reinforcing the belief that you are worthy of investment and capable of achieving greatness. This self-confidence becomes a cornerstone upon which you can build a life of purpose and fulfillment.

Quality of Life Enhanced:

Imagine the ripple effects of dedicating yourself to a four-day workout routine. With each session, you're not just building muscle or burning calories; you're investing in a life of vitality and joy. Research consistently demonstrates that individuals who engage in regular exercise report higher levels of energy, improved sleep quality, and enhanced overall well-being. By prioritizing your physical health through consistent movement, you're unlocking the key to a life of boundless energy and endless possibilities.

Furthermore, the social aspect of exercise cannot be overstated. Whether you're hitting the gym with a workout buddy or joining a group fitness class, regular exercise provides invaluable opportunities for connection and camaraderie. These social bonds not only enrich your workouts but also spill over into other areas of your life, fostering a sense of belonging and community that is essential for holistic well-being.

Identifying Patterns and Progress:

Tracking your workouts provides invaluable insight into your fitness journey, allowing you to identify patterns, strengths, and areas for growth. By documenting details such as exercise duration, intensity, and performance metrics, you gain a deeper understanding of what works best for your body and how to optimize your training regimen for maximum results.

Moreover, tracking your progress over time enables you to set realistic goals and measure your success along the way. Whether it's aiming to increase your strength, improve your endurance, or achieve a specific fitness milestone, having concrete data at your fingertips empowers you to make informed decisions and track your journey toward success.

Staying Accountable and Consistent:

Consistency is the cornerstone of any successful fitness journey, and documenting your workouts can help you stay accountable to your goals. By committing to record each workout session, you're creating a sense of accountability to yourself and your aspirations. This simple act of accountability can make all the difference on those days when motivation wanes and excuses tempt you to skip a workout.

Furthermore, sharing your progress with a supportive community of like-minded individuals can provide additional accountability and encouragement. Whether it's through social media, online forums, or workout buddies, knowing that others are cheering you on can inspire you to stay consistent and committed to your fitness goals.

Embracing the Journey:

Take a journey with me

By capturing the highs and lows, the victories and setbacks, you're creating a living record of your fitness journey—one that reflects not only your physical strength but also your resilience, determination, and unwavering commitment to self-improvement.

Exercise Log

Keeping an exercise log is like keeping a diary of your efforts to stay healthy. Each entry captures every detail of your workout session—such as the exercises you performed, the number of sets and repetitions, and the equipment you utilized. By maintaining this record, you demonstrate your commitment to your physical well-being, cultivating a sense of fulfillment that bolsters your resilience during challenging times.

By diligently documenting your workouts, you not only track your fitness journey but also cultivate a deeper connection with your body and mind. Whether you're striving to achieve specific fitness goals or simply aiming to lead a healthier lifestyle, maintaining an exercise log can be a powerful tool for success. So grab a pen and paper, or fire up your favorite fitness app, and start logging your workouts today. Your body and mind will thank you for it.

Workout Log Template:

Date:

_____

Describe Exercise

_____

Note Position or Form

_____

Number of Sets

_____

Number of Repetitions

_____

Specify Equipment or Tools

Proverbs 17:22 states, "A joyful heart is good medicine, but a crushed spirit dries up the bones." Including a scripture about joy and healing, such as Proverbs 17:22, can add a spiritual dimension to your fitness journey. This verse emphasizes the connection between a joyful heart and good health, underscoring the importance of maintaining a positive mindset as we strive to improve our physical well-being.

Personal Experience:

Main Body:

Conclusion:

Importance of Rest

Rest is crucial for maintaining your overall well-being. It's akin to a comforting tune that plays a vital role in self-care, offering a respite for both your mind and body. While it might seem like a simple concept, the significance of rest cannot be overstated.

First and foremost, rest allows your body to recharge and recuperate. Just as a battery needs to be recharged to function optimally, your body requires rest to restore its energy levels. When you rest, your muscles relax, your heart rate slows down, and your breathing becomes deeper and more regular. This downtime is essential for repairing tissues, replenishing energy stores, and promoting overall physical health.

Moreover, rest plays a crucial role in mental well-being. In today's fast-paced world, our minds are constantly bombarded with stimuli, leading to stress and mental fatigue. Taking time to rest provides an opportunity to unwind and clear your thoughts. It allows your mind to relax, reduces stress levels, and promotes mental clarity. Just like a cluttered room needs tidying up to create space, your mind benefits from rest to declutter and rejuvenate.

In addition to its physical, mental, and emotional benefits, rest also fosters creativity and innovation. When you're well-rested, your mind is free to wander and explore new ideas. Rest provides the space for inspiration to flourish and creativity to thrive. Many great inventions and breakthroughs have occurred during moments of rest and relaxation, highlighting the profound connection between rest and creativity.

Moreover, rest is essential for maintaining healthy relationships. When you're rested and rejuvenated, you're better equipped to connect with others empathetically and communicate effectively. Conversely, sleep deprivation can lead to irritability and conflict in relationships. By prioritizing rest, you can nurture and strengthen your connections with others, fostering healthier and more fulfilling relationships.

Importance of sleep in maintaining a healthy lifestyle

Getting enough sleep is crucial for a healthy life. It's like recharging your body and mind for the day ahead. When you sleep well, you feel better, think clearer, and have more energy. But why is sleep so important, and how can you make sure you're getting enough of it?

Firstly, sleep plays a vital role in your physical health. It gives your body a chance to repair and rejuvenate itself. While you sleep, your body produces hormones that help repair cells and tissues, boosting your immune system and keeping you healthy. Not getting enough sleep can weaken your immune system, making you more susceptible to illness and infections.

Moreover, sleep is essential for your mental well-being. It's during sleep that your brain processes information, consolidates memories, and clears out toxins. This helps improve your cognitive function, concentration, and productivity during the day. When you're well-rested, you're better equipped to handle stress and regulate your emotions, leading to better overall mental health.

Additionally, sleep plays a crucial role in regulating your appetite and weight. Lack of sleep disrupts the balance of hormones that control hunger and satiety, leading to increased cravings for high-calorie foods and a higher risk of weight gain. On the other hand, getting enough sleep helps maintain a healthy metabolism and reduces the likelihood of overeating.

Furthermore, sleep is essential for your cardiovascular health. Chronic sleep deprivation has been linked to an increased risk of heart disease, hypertension, and stroke. During sleep, your blood pressure and heart rate naturally decrease, giving your cardiovascular system a chance to rest and recover. Consistently getting enough sleep can help lower your risk of developing these serious health conditions.

So, how can you ensure you're getting enough quality sleep? Start by establishing a regular sleep schedule and sticking to it, even on weekends. Create a relaxing bedtime routine to signal to your body that it's time to wind down. This could include activities like reading, taking a warm bath, or practicing relaxation techniques like deep breathing or meditation. Avoid stimulants like caffeine and electronics before bedtime, as they can interfere with your ability to fall asleep.

Make sure your sleep environment is conducive to rest by keeping your bedroom cool, dark, and quiet. Invest in a comfortable mattress and pillows that support your body and help reduce any discomfort that might disrupt your sleep. Limit exposure to screens emitting blue light, as it can suppress the production of melatonin, the hormone that regulates sleep-wake cycles.

If you're struggling to sleep due to stress, anxiety, or other underlying issues, consider seeking help from a healthcare professional. They can offer guidance and support to address any sleep disorders or concerns that may be affecting your ability to rest well.

In conclusion, sleep is not just a luxury but a necessity for maintaining a healthy lifestyle. It's essential for physical health, mental well-being, weight management, and cardiovascular health. By prioritizing sleep and adopting healthy sleep habits, you can improve your overall quality of life and reduce your risk of numerous health problems. So, tonight, make a commitment to prioritize your sleep and reap the many benefits it has to offer.

Emphasis on the role of rest in recovery and performance

We all know the value of hard work. Pushing ourselves to strive for improvement – these are cornerstones of success. But what if there's a hidden ingredient, often overlooked, that unlocks our full potential? That ingredient is rest.

Science confirms that rest isn't just about taking a breather; it's the foundation for peak performance, both physically and mentally. Here's how prioritizing rest can supercharge your recovery and propel you towards your goals.

How Rest Rebuilds Your Body?

Think of your body as a high-performance machine. During exercise, you stress your muscles, causing microscopic tears. Rest provides the crucial window for repair. Studies show that during sleep, growth hormone production increases significantly. This hormone plays a vital role in muscle repair and tissue regeneration. Skimping on rest hinders this process, leaving you feeling sore and hindering progress.

Rest also allows your body to replenish glycogen, the fuel your muscles use for energy. A 2013 study published in the Medicine & Science in Sports & Exercise journal found that athletes who prioritized sleep recovery for just one week saw a significant increase in muscle glycogen stores, leading to improved endurance performance.

Beyond the Body: Rest and Mental Sharpness

The benefits of rest extend far beyond the physical. When you're well-rested, your brain functions at its peak. Studies have shown that sleep deprivation negatively impacts cognitive function, memory, and reaction time. A well-rested mind is sharper, more focused, and better at problem-solving – all crucial for peak performance in any field.

Listen to Your Body: The Art of Restful Recovery

So, how much rest is enough? The truth is it varies depending on your individual needs and activity level. However, there are some key indicators your body sends when it craves rest:

Persistent fatigue: Feeling constantly drained is a red flag.

Decreased motivation: Pushing through exhaustion can zap your enthusiasm and motivation.

Increased injury risk: A fatigued body is more susceptible to injuries.

Diminished performance: Notice a drop in your workouts or daily activities? It might be a sign you need a break.

Making Rest a Priority: Practical Tips for Recharging

Rest in your daily routine for optimal recovery:

Prioritize sleep: Aim for 7-8 hours of quality sleep each night. Create a relaxing bedtime routine and stick to a consistent sleep schedule.

Schedule rest days: Don't push yourself to exercise every day. Include active recovery days with light activities like yoga or walking to promote blood flow and muscle repair.

Listen to your body: Pay attention to your fatigue levels and adjust your training intensity or duration accordingly.

De-stress techniques: Techniques like meditation or deep breathing can help manage stress hormones, which can interfere with sleep and recovery.

Disconnect to recharge: Set boundaries with technology. Avoid screens before bed and carve out time for activities that help you unwind.

Rest: The Unsung Hero of Peak Performance

Remember, rest isn't a sign of weakness; it's a sign of strength and strategic planning. By prioritizing rest, you're giving your body and mind the tools they need to recover, rebuild, and perform at their absolute best. So, embrace rest as your secret weapon – it's the key to unlocking your full potential and achieving sustainable success.

How Morning Journaling Can Charge Your Day

We all have dreams, goals, and a desire to be the best versions of ourselves. But between the daily grind and the constant stream of thoughts, it can be easy to lose sight of these aspirations.

Here's where a simple practice – morning journaling – can play a transformative role in self-reflection, goal setting, and, ultimately, self-improvement.

Why Mornings Matter:

The first moments after waking hold immense power. Our minds are relatively clear, uncluttered by the day's accumulated stress and distractions. This makes it the perfect time to tap into our inner selves and set intentions for a productive and fulfilling day. Journaling in the morning allows you to:

Gain Clarity: As you write, jumbled thoughts begin to take shape. You can identify priorities, anxieties, and goals that may have been lingering subconsciously. This clarity allows you to approach the day with a focused mind.

Embrace Gratitude: Starting your day by reflecting on things you're grateful for sets a positive tone. Research shows gratitude can enhance mood, reduce stress, and even improve sleep [1]. Journaling about what you appreciate sets a foundation for optimism and well-being.

Set Intentions: Instead of being swept away by the day's demands, journaling allows you to define your own direction. Write down your goals for the day, both big and small. This simple act of intention setting increases your focus and the likelihood of achieving them.

Tailoring Your Morning Journaling Practice

Morning journaling is a flexible tool. Here are some ways to customize it to your specific needs:

27

Gratitude Journaling: List down 3-5 things you're grateful for, big or small. It could be your health, family, a good cup of coffee, or anything that brings you joy.

Goal Setting: Write down specific, measurable, achievable, relevant, and time-bound (SMART) goals for the day. This could be anything from finishing a work project to spending quality time with loved ones.

Affirmation Journaling: Write down positive statements about yourself and your abilities. Repeating affirmations reinforces self-belief and boosts confidence.

Mindfulness Journaling: Reflect on your emotions and thought patterns without judgment. Observe any recurring worries or negative self-talk and challenge them with more positive perspectives.

Brain Dump: Sometimes, you just need to get everything out of your head. Jot down fleeting thoughts, to-do lists, or worries. This clearing of the mental clutter can free up space for focused thinking throughout the day.

Morning Journaling Practical Tips for Success

Like any new habit, establishing a consistent morning journaling routine takes dedication. Here are some tips to help you stick with it:

Start Small: Aim for just 5-10 minutes of journaling in the morning. Gradually increase the time as your routine becomes more established.

Find Your Perfect Spot: Choose a quiet, comfortable space where you won't be interrupted.

Embrace the Tools: Whether it's a pen and paper notebook or a journaling app, find what works best for you.

Schedule It In: Treat journaling like an important appointment. Set a reminder and stick to it as much as possible.

Don't Worry About Perfection: There are no right or wrong ways to journal. Focus on free-flowing expression and authentic self-reflection.

The Power of Consistency

The real magic of morning journaling unfolds over time. As you build this practice into your routine, you'll start to notice a shift:

Improved Self-Awareness: Journaling helps you gain a deeper understanding of your strengths, weaknesses, and triggers. This self-awareness empowers you to make positive changes in your life.

Enhanced Problem-Solving: By regularly reflecting on challenges, you develop better problem-solving skills. Journaling provides a space to brainstorm solutions and identify new ways to approach obstacles.

Increased Productivity: A clear mind and defined goals lead to better time management and increased productivity.

Greater Resilience: Journaling can be a powerful tool for managing stress and negative emotions. By acknowledging and processing your feelings, you become better equipped to handle challenges and overcome setbacks.

A Simple Path to a Fulfilling Life

Starting your day with a few minutes of self-reflection sets you on a path to greater self-awareness, goal achievement, and, ultimately, self-improvement. It's an easy practice to incorporate into your routine, yet the benefits are far-reaching. So grab a pen, find a quiet space, and unlock the power of morning journaling.

Rest and Reflect

_____

_____

_____

_____

_____

_____

_____

_____

_____

_____

_____

_____

_____

_____

_____

_____

_____

Take a journey with me

_____

_____

_____

_____

_____

_____

_____

_____

_____

Nutritional Guidance

Imagine your body as a complex orchestra. Each instrument, from the powerful brass to the delicate flutes, plays a crucial role in creating beautiful music. Similarly, our bodies rely on a harmonious interplay of nutrients to function optimally. Nutrition, the science of food and its impact on health serves as the conductor of this symphony, ensuring all the instruments – our organs, tissues, and cells – receive the right notes to perform flawlessly.

Macronutrients and Micronutrients

Just as a symphony relies on a variety of instruments, our bodies require a diverse range of nutrients. These can be broadly categorized into two groups: macronutrients and micronutrients.

Macronutrients: These are the workhorses of the body, providing energy to fuel our daily activities. They include:

Carbohydrates: The body's primary source of readily available energy. Carbs come in two main forms: simple carbs (found in sugary foods) and complex carbs (found in whole grains, fruits, and vegetables).

Proteins: Essential for building and repairing tissues, proteins are the building blocks of life. They are found in animal sources like meat and fish, as well as plant-based sources like legumes and nuts.

Fats: Often demonized, healthy fats are crucial for hormone production, cell function, and brain health. Sources of healthy fats include avocados, nuts, olive oil, and fatty fish.

Micronutrients: While they may be smaller in quantity, micronutrients play a vital role in regulating bodily processes. These include:

Vitamins: Essential for various functions, from maintaining healthy vision (vitamin A) to supporting the immune system (vitamin C).

Minerals: Needed for strong bones and teeth (calcium), proper nerve function (sodium, potassium), and oxygen transport (iron).

Building a Balanced Plate

So how do we ensure our internal orchestra receives the right blend of "notes"? The answer lies in a balanced diet. Here are some key principles to adopt:

Variety is Key: Include a range of foods from all food groups (fruits, vegetables, whole grains, lean protein sources, and healthy fats) on your plate. This diversity ensures you're getting a broad spectrum of nutrients.

Focus on Whole Foods: Prioritize whole, unprocessed foods over refined ones. Whole foods are packed with more nutrients and fiber, which keeps you feeling fuller for longer.

Portion Control: Moderation is key. While all foods can be part of a healthy diet, mindful portion control helps manage calorie intake and prevent overeating.

Don't Forget Hydration: Water is essential for every bodily function. Aim for 8 glasses of water per day to stay hydrated and support optimal health.

Factors Influencing Nutrition

Nutrition is more than just the food we eat. Several other factors play a role:

Lifestyle: Physical activity level, sleep patterns, and stress management all influence your nutritional needs.

Individual Needs: Age, gender, and health conditions can all influence the specific nutrients your body requires.

Cultural Influences: Food choices are often shaped by cultural traditions and preferences.

The Takeaway

By understanding the principles of good nutrition and making informed dietary choices, you empower your body to perform at its best. Just like a well-conducted orchestra creates beautiful music, a balanced diet provides the foundation for a healthy and fulfilling life. Remember, nutrition is a journey, not a destination. Experiment, find what works best for you, and enjoy the process of nourishing your body for lifelong well-being.

The Art of Meal Planning

Meal planning isn't about restriction; it's about creating a roadmap for a healthy and enjoyable week. Here's why it's a valuable tool:

Saves Time and Money: Planning helps you avoid last-minute unhealthy choices and impulse grocery purchases. You can create a grocery list based on your planned meals, leading to cost-effective shopping.

Promotes Variety: Meal planning encourages you to explore a wider range of nutritious ingredients and recipes, ensuring a well-balanced diet.

Reduces Food Waste: Buying only what you need reduces the likelihood of food spoilage and wasted money.

Stress-Free Meal Preparation: Knowing what's for dinner eliminates the daily scramble of "what to cook." You can even prep ingredients in advance for a smoother cooking experience.

Crafting Your Weekly Menu: Essential Elements

Now, let's get started on building your meal plan. Here's what to consider:

Balance for Every Meal: Aim for a plate that incorporates different food groups – carbohydrates for energy (whole grains, fruits), protein for building and repairing tissues (lean meats, fish, beans), healthy fats for satiety and cell function (avocados, nuts, olive oil), and vegetables for essential vitamins and minerals.

Consider Dietary Needs: Do you have any allergies or dietary restrictions? Vegan, vegetarian, gluten-free – tailor your plan to your specific needs.

Seasonal and Local Produce: Opt for fresh, seasonal ingredients whenever possible. This promotes sustainability and often leads to more flavorful dishes.

Meal Prep Strategies: Certain meals can be prepped in advance to save time during the week. Consider pre-chopping vegetables, cooking grains in bulk, or marinating proteins for easy assembly later.

Building a Recipe Repertoire

With your meal plan in place, it's time to explore the world of healthy recipes! Here are some strategies to find inspiration:

Cookbooks and Online Resources: Countless cookbooks and websites offer an abundance of healthy recipes. Look for options that cater to your dietary preferences and cooking skills.

Simple Twists on Familiar Dishes: Take your favorite comfort foods and give them a healthy makeover. Swap white rice for brown rice, use lean protein sources, and add plenty of vegetables to boost nutrient content.

Theme Nights: Spice up your week with themed nights. Meatless Mondays, Taco Tuesdays, or International Food Fridays can add variety and fun to your meal plan.

Experimentation is Key: Don't be afraid to try new ingredients and recipes. The more you explore, the more you'll discover healthy and delicious favorites.

From Planning to Plate

Meal planning and exploring recipes are not about perfection; they're about taking control of your health and well-being in a delicious way. Start with small changes, gradually incorporate new ingredients, and celebrate your culinary creations. Remember, a healthy and vibrant life is like a beautiful painting – it's built stroke by stroke, with each meal adding its own unique flavor and nourishment to your personal masterpiece.

Smart Snacking and Hydration Strategies

Eating healthy isn't just about what you have for breakfast, lunch, and dinner. Snacks play a crucial role in maintaining energy levels, curbing cravings, and ensuring you reach your daily nutritional goals. This, coupled with adequate hydration, forms the foundation for a healthy and well-functioning body.

The Power of Snacking: Why Smart Choices Matter

Here's why incorporating smart snacks into your routine is beneficial:

Sustained Energy Levels: Spaced-out meals with appropriate snacks prevent blood sugar crashes that can lead to fatigue and cravings.

Nutrient Boost: Snacks can help fill nutritional gaps, especially if you struggle to meet your daily requirements through meals alone.

Appetite Control: Healthy snacks can prevent overeating at meals by keeping you feeling satisfied throughout the day.

Enhanced Performance: Smart snacking choices can improve focus, concentration, and even physical performance during workouts.

Building a Snacking Arsenal

Not all snacks are created equal. Here are some healthy and satisfying snack ideas to consider:

Fresh Fruit with Nut Butter: A classic combination, fruits provide natural sugars for energy, while nut butter offers healthy fats and protein for sustained satiety.

Veggies with Hummus: Dip sliced bell peppers, carrots, or cucumbers into hummus for a fiber-rich and protein-packed snack.

Greek Yogurt with Berries: Greek yogurt offers a good dose of protein and calcium, while berries add a burst of antioxidants and sweetness.

Hard-boiled Eggs: A convenient and portable source of protein and healthy fats, hard-boiled eggs are a great mid-morning or afternoon snack.

Trail Mix: Make your own trail mix with nuts, seeds, and dried fruits for a balanced snack that curbs hunger pangs.

Edamame: This boiled or roasted soybean option packs a protein punch and provides essential vitamins and minerals.

Homemade Energy Bites: Combine rolled oats, nut butter, honey, and dried fruit for a delicious and energy-boosting snack.

The Importance of Hydration

Water is the lifeblood of our body. Every cell, tissue, and organ relies on it to function properly. Here's why staying hydrated is crucial:

Regulates Body Temperature: Water helps regulate body temperature, preventing overheating during exercise or hot weather.

Lubricates Joints: Proper hydration keeps joints lubricated, promoting flexibility and reducing the risk of injury.

Aids Digestion: Drinking enough water helps move food through the digestive system, preventing constipation and bloating.

Boosts Brain Function: Dehydration can negatively impact cognitive function, focus, and memory.

Supports Overall Health: Adequate water intake is essential for optimal physical and mental health.

Staying Hydrated

Making water your go-to beverage is the foundation of good hydration. Here are some tips to ensure you meet your daily fluid needs:

Carry a Reusable Water Bottle: Having a water bottle with you throughout the day serves as a constant reminder to drink.

Set Hydration Goals: Aim for 8 glasses of water per day, adjusting based on your activity level and climate.

Infuse Your Water: Add slices of cucumber, lemon, or berries to your water for a refreshing and flavorful twist.

Choose Water-Rich Foods: Fruits and vegetables like watermelon, cucumber, and celery are high in water content, contributing to your daily intake.

Listen to Your Body: Pay attention to thirst cues, and don't wait until you feel dehydrated to drink water.

The Final Sip

By incorporating smart snacking and mindful hydration habits into your daily routine, you're not just nourishing your body; you're empowering it to thrive. Choose snacks that are both delicious and nutritious and prioritize water as your beverage of choice. Remember, small changes consistently applied lead to big results. Make these practices a part of your lifestyle and watch your energy levels, focus, and overall well-being soar.

Mental Health and Motivation

Our journey toward a healthier lifestyle begins not on the gym floor or in the kitchen but within the workshop of our minds. It's here that our dreams, goals, and determination take root. Cultivating a positive mindset is the cornerstone of motivation, resilience, and, ultimately, success in any endeavor, including health and well-being.

Why Mindset Matters

Our mindset – the collection of beliefs and attitudes we hold – plays a crucial role in shaping our behavior. Here's why a positive mindset is essential for achieving your health goals:

Empowers Positive Action: When you believe in your ability to succeed, you're more likely to take action and persevere through challenges.

Boosts Motivation: A positive mindset fuels motivation, the driving force that gets you started and keeps you going on your health journey.

Improves Resilience: Setbacks are inevitable. A positive mindset allows you to bounce back from setbacks and keep moving forward.

Reduces Stress: Negative thoughts and self-doubt can contribute to stress. A positive mindset promotes a sense of calm and control.

Enhances Self-Compassion: Positive self-talk fosters self-compassion, allowing you to learn from mistakes and stay motivated despite imperfections.

Shifting Your Perspective

The good news is that our mindset isn't fixed. Here are some tools to cultivate a positive mindset for your health journey:

Set SMART Goals: Specific, Measurable, Achievable, Relevant, and Time-bound goals are more attainable and create a sense of accomplishment.

Focus on Progress, Not Perfection: Celebrate small victories along the way. Progress, not perfection, is the key to long-term success.

Practice Positive Self-Talk: Replace negative self-criticism with encouraging affirmations. Talk to yourself the way you would talk to a supportive friend.

Visualization: Imagine yourself achieving your health goals. Visualization helps solidify your goals and increase motivation.

Reframe Challenges as Opportunities: View setbacks as opportunities to learn and grow.

Gratitude Practice: Focusing on the things you're grateful for fosters a positive outlook and boosts motivation.

Surround Yourself with Positive Influences: Spend time with people who support your health goals and uplift your spirits.

Overcoming Obstacles

Even with a positive mindset, challenges will arise. Here's how to cultivate resilience:

Anticipate Setbacks: Know that setbacks are part of the journey. Don't let them derail your progress.

Focus on Controllables: Focus on what you can control – your effort, your attitude, and your choices. Don't dwell on things outside your control.

Learn from Mistakes: Every setback holds a lesson. Analyze what went wrong and adjust your approach for the next time.

Celebrate Recovery: Acknowledge your strength in bouncing back from challenges.

Seek Support: Don't be afraid to reach out to friends, family, or a therapist for support and encouragement.

Your Mind-Body Connection

When it comes to health and well-being, your mind and body are interconnected. By cultivating a positive mindset, you unlock the power to make lasting changes, overcome obstacles, and achieve your health goals. Remember, a positive mindset is a journey, not a destination. There will be ups and downs, but by consistently practicing these strategies, you'll build an inner champion that empowers you to reach your full potential and live a healthier, happier life.

Cultivating Practices for a Flourishing Life

Self-care isn't a luxury; it's the foundation for a healthy and fulfilling life. Just as a plant withers without proper nourishment, we can't thrive without tending to our physical, mental, and emotional needs. This guide explores various self-care practices, empowering you to create a personalized toolkit for well-being.

The Power of Positive Affirmations

Our inner voice can be our greatest cheerleader or harshest critic. Affirmations – positive statements that reinforce our self-belief – can be a powerful tool for cultivating a growth mindset and fostering motivation.

How Affirmations Work:

Reprogramming the Subconscious: By repeating affirmations regularly, we begin to reprogram our subconscious mind, replacing negative self-talk with empowering beliefs.

Shifting Focus: Affirmations direct our attention towards our strengths and potential, creating a positive outlook and promoting goal achievement.

Boosting Confidence: Positive self-talk enhances self-confidence, making us more likely to take risks and step outside our comfort zones.

Crafting Your Affirmations:

Focus on "I Am": Start with "I am" followed by a positive quality you want to cultivate, such as "I am confident," "I am capable," or "I am worthy."

Personalize Your Statements: Choose affirmations that resonate with your current goals and aspirations.

Present Tense is Key: Frame your affirmations in the present tense, emphasizing your existing strengths and potential.

Repetition is Power: Repeat your affirmations daily, either silently or aloud, to solidify their impact on your mindset.

Examples of Affirmations:

* "I am strong and capable of achieving anything I set my mind to."

* "I am worthy of love and happiness."

* "I am resilient and can overcome any challenge."

* "I embrace healthy habits and make choices that nourish my body and mind."

The Encouragement Within: Building a Support System

Self-care isn't a solo endeavor. Surrounding yourself with a supportive network can provide invaluable encouragement and act as a safety net during challenging times.

Building Your Support System:

Identify Your Tribe: Connect with friends, family members, or colleagues who uplift and motivate you.

Seek Professional Help: Consider therapy or coaching for guidance on self-improvement and navigating personal challenges.

Join a Community: Find online or in-person communities focused on shared interests or goals.

The Power of Reflection and Gratitude

Taking time for reflection allows you to appreciate your progress, identify areas for improvement, and gain valuable insights about yourself. Gratitude, the act of appreciating what you have, fosters a positive outlook and boosts well-being.

The Benefits of Reflection

Celebrating Victories: Acknowledge your accomplishments, big or small. This reinforces positive behavior and motivates you to keep moving forward.

Learning from Challenges: Setbacks happen. Reflect on what went wrong and use these lessons to build resilience and improve your approach.

Setting Goals: Regular reflection helps you identify areas you want to focus on and set clear, achievable goals for personal growth.

The Power of Gratitude

Increased Happiness: Gratitude practices have been shown to enhance mood and overall well-being.

Improved Relationships: Appreciating others strengthens relationships and fosters a sense of connection.

Savoring the Good: Focusing on gratitude allows you to appreciate the good things in your life, even the small ones, creating a more fulfilling experience.

Keeping a Gratitude Journal:

Daily Practice: Dedicate a few minutes each day to write down things you're grateful for. These can be big things like good health or small things like a delicious meal.

Specificity is Key: The more specific you are, the more impactful your gratitude practice will be.

Reflect and Savor: Take a moment to truly appreciate what you're grateful for.

Remember: Self-care is a journey, not a destination. Experiment with different practices, find what works best for you, and refine your approach over time. By incorporating affirmations, building a support system, practicing reflection, and cultivating gratitude, you'll cultivate a flourishing life that empowers you to reach your full potential.

Conclusion and Next Steps

We've embarked on a transformative journey, exploring the pillars of a healthy and fulfilling life. You've learned about the power of rest, the importance of balanced nutrition, the tools for mindful snacking and hydration, the influence of mindset and motivation, and the essential practices of self-care. As we reach the end of this chapter, let's celebrate your accomplishments and acknowledge the exciting path ahead.

Celebrating Your Progress:

Reflect on Your Wins: Take a moment to appreciate the positive changes you've made, big or small. Did you incorporate more fruits and vegetables into your diet? Did you establish a regular sleep schedule? Celebrate these victories!

Take a journey with me

_____

_____

_____

_____

Acknowledge Challenges: Growth rarely happens without obstacles. Look back at the challenges you faced and recognize the strength and resilience you displayed in overcoming them.

Take a journey with me

Recommended reading list

Here is a curated selection of literature that delves deeper into the realms of health, wellness, and personal development:

Eat This Much: Personalized Meal Plans for Sustainable Weight Loss by Leanne Brown, RD

This book is a great resource for anyone looking to lose weight or improve their eating habits. It provides personalized meal plans based on your individual needs and goals. Brown is a registered dietitian who has helped thousands of people lose weight and keep it off.

The How Not to Die Cookbook by Michael Greger, MD

This book is a companion to Dr. Greger's popular book, "How Not to Die." It provides over 100 recipes that are designed to help you prevent and reverse chronic diseases. The recipes are all plant-based and are packed with nutrients.

Spark: The Revolutionary New Science of Exercise and the Brain by John Ratey, MD

This book explores the latest science on how exercise can improve your brain health. Ratey, a psychiatrist, argues that exercise is essential for cognitive function, mood, and overall well-being.

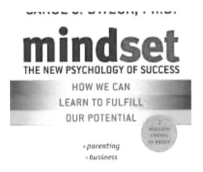

Mindset: The New Psychology of Success by Carol Dweck

This book explores the concept of mindset and how it can impact your success in life. Dweck, a psychologist, argues that there are two main mindsets: a fixed mindset and a growth mindset. People with a fixed mindset believe that their intelligence and abilities are fixed, while people with a growth mindset believe that they can learn and grow. Dweck's book shows how you can develop a growth mindset and achieve your goals.

The Happiness Project by Gretchen Rubin

This book is a memoir by Gretchen Rubin, who decided to spend a year testing out different happiness philosophies. Rubin's book is a fun and engaging read that will give you some ideas for how to boost your own happiness.

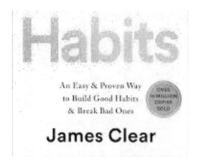

Atomic Habits by James Clear

This book is all about how to create and stick to good habits. Clear, a behavioral scientist, argues that small changes can lead to big results over time. His book provides a practical framework for building good habits and breaking bad ones.

You Are a Badass: How to Stop Doubting Your Greatness and Start Living an Awesome Life by Jen Sincero

This book is a self-help book that will help you to overcome your fears and start living your best life. Sincero's book is full of practical advice and inspirational stories.

The Power of Vulnerability by Brené Brown

This book is about the importance of vulnerability in our lives. Brown, a social scientist, argues that vulnerability is the key to connection, creativity, and love. Her book will help you to embrace your vulnerability and live a more authentic life.

I hope this curated selection helps you on your journey to a healthier, happier, and more fulfilling life!

Space for additional notes or reflections

Theresa Mitchell

Take a journey with me

_____

_____

_____

_____

_____

_____

_____

_____

_____

_____

_____

Exercises

Expanding Your Fitness Horizons: Exercises to Challenge and Invigorate

Your fitness journey shouldn't be monotonous! Here's a selection of exercises designed to challenge different muscle groups and keep your workouts exciting:

High-Intensity Interval Training (HIIT):

Burpees: This full-body exercise combines a squat, push-up, and jump for an intense cardio burst.

Jump Squats: Add an explosive jump to your squat routine to elevate your heart rate and target your lower body.

Mountain Climbers: Engage your core and legs with this dynamic exercise that simulates climbing a mountain.

Strength Training:

Single-leg Deadlifts: Challenge your balance and core stability while strengthening your hamstrings and glutes.

Turkish Get-Ups: This complex movement works your entire body, from core to shoulders, requiring coordination and strength.

Push-up Variations: From incline push-ups to diamond push-ups, there are numerous variations to target different muscle groups in your chest, shoulders, and triceps.

Bodyweight Exercises:

Plank Variations: Planks are a fantastic core exercise. Experiment with high planks, low planks, and side planks to target different core muscles.

Dips: Utilize benches, chairs, or dip bars to build upper body strength, targeting your chest, triceps, and shoulders.

Lunges with Overhead Reach: This lunge variation adds an upper-body challenge to work your legs and core simultaneously.

Functional Fitness:

Medicine Ball Slams: Engage your core and upper body muscles with explosive slams of a medicine ball.

Box Jumps: Challenge your power and explosiveness by jumping onto a stable box.

Kettlebell Swings: This dynamic exercise works your core, legs, and back, mimicking a swinging motion with a kettlebell.

Yoga and Pilates:

Vinyasa Yoga: This flowing style of yoga focuses on linking breath with movement, improving coordination and flexibility.

Iyengar Yoga: This style utilizes props like blocks and straps to enhance alignment and deepen poses.

Pilates: Pilates focuses on core strength, improving posture, flexibility, and stability.

Remember:

Warm-Up and Cool-Down: Always begin your workout with a dynamic warm-up and end with a static cool-down to prevent injuries.

Listen to Your Body: Start slow, gradually increase intensity, and don't hesitate to modify exercises as needed.

Seek Guidance: Consider consulting a certified personal trainer for personalized workout plans and proper form guidance.

Remember, consistency is key. Find what you enjoy and make physical activity a regular part of your life for a healthier and happier you!

Recipes

Embark on a delicious journey filled with vibrant flavors and wholesome ingredients! These recipes cater to various dietary preferences and are designed to fuel your body throughout the day.

Breakfast Delights:

Power Smoothie Bowl: Blend Greek yogurt, frozen berries, spinach, and a drizzle of honey for a protein-packed and refreshing breakfast. Top with granola, chia seeds, and sliced almonds for extra crunch and texture. (Vegan option: use plant-based yogurt)

Scrambled Eggs with Smoked Salmon and Avocado: A classic with a twist! Scramble eggs with chopped onions and peppers, then top with smoked salmon slices and creamy avocado for a satisfying and healthy breakfast.

Whole-Wheat Pancakes with Berries and Nuts: Ditch the sugary pancake mixes and whip up a batch of fluffy whole-wheat pancakes. Top them with fresh berries, chopped nuts, and a drizzle of maple syrup for a sweet and satisfying start to your day.

Lunchtime Feasts:

Quinoa Salad with Roasted Vegetables: This protein-rich salad is perfect for a light and flavorful lunch. Combine quinoa with roasted vegetables like broccoli, sweet potato, and red onion. Dress with a lemon-tahini sauce for a tangy and flavorful touch. (Vegan)

Tuna Salad Sandwich on Whole-Wheat Bread: This classic gets a healthy upgrade. Mix canned tuna with chopped celery, red onion, and a light yogurt-based dressing. Pile it high on whole-wheat bread for a satisfying and protein-rich lunch.

Lentil Soup with Whole-Grain Bread: This hearty soup is packed with protein and fiber. Simmer lentils with vegetables like carrots, celery, and tomatoes for a delicious and comforting lunch. Pair it with a slice of whole-grain bread for a complete meal. (Vegan)

Dinner Delights:

Salmon with Roasted Brussels Sprouts and Quinoa: This dish is a well-balanced combination of protein, vegetables, and whole grains. Roast Brussels sprouts with olive oil and spices, bake salmon seasoned with herbs, and serve overcooked quinoa for a nutritious and flavorful meal.

Chicken Stir-Fry with Brown Rice: A quick and easy weeknight dinner option. Stir-fried chicken strips with colorful vegetables like broccoli, snap peas, and bell peppers. Serve over brown rice for a satisfying and complete meal.

Vegetarian Chili: A hearty and comforting dish perfect for a cozy night in. Simmer black beans, kidney beans, corn, diced tomatoes, and spices for a flavorful chili. Top with chopped avocado, shredded cheese (optional), and a dollop of Greek yogurt for a complete and satisfying meal. (Vegetarians can be made vegan by omitting cheese and yogurt)

Satisfying Snacks:

Trail Mix: A convenient and portable source of protein and healthy fats. Combine nuts, seeds, dried fruit, and dark chocolate chips for a delicious and energy-boosting snack.

Vegetable Sticks with Hummus: Dip sliced carrots, cucumbers, and bell peppers into creamy hummus for a satisfying and healthy snack.

Greek Yogurt with Berries and Granola: A classic snack option packed with protein, fiber, and antioxidants. Layer Greek yogurt with fresh berries and a sprinkle of granola for a delicious and nutritious treat.

Remember, these are just a starting point! Explore different cuisines, experiment with flavors, and find healthy recipes that tantalize your taste buds and nourish your body. With a little creativity, you can enjoy delicious and nutritious meals at every stage of your day.

Thank you so much for starting this journey with me I am so proud of you. There is a whole series of Journey journals to come so stick around and continue to be a part of a helpful and meaningful community. God bless

Made in United States
Troutdale, OR
09/18/2024